THE BATTLE OF MARATHON

The Decisive End to the First Greco-Persian War

Written by Delphine Dumont
In collaboration with Nicolas Cartelet
Translated by Carly Probert

History | 50MINUTES.com

THE BATTLE OF MARATHON

KEY INFORMATION

- **When:** 13 September 490 B.C.
- **Where:** Marathon (Greece)
- **Context:** The Greco-Persian Wars (490-479 B.C.)
- **Belligerents:** Athens and Plataea (city of Boeotia) against the Persian Empire
- **Commanders and leaders:**
  - Miltiades, Athenian strategist (550-489 B.C.)
  - Callimachus of Aphidna, Athenian polemarch (6th century-498 B.C.)
  - Datis the Mede, Persian admiral (late 6th century-early 5th century B.C.)
  - Artaphernes, Persian general (late 6th century-early 5th century B.C.)
- **Outcome:** Greek victory
- **Victims:**
  - Greek side: approximately 192 dead
  - Persian side: approximately 6 400 dead

INTRODUCTION

A decisive victory of the Greeks over the Persian forces, the Battle of Marathon ended the first Greco-Persian war in 490 B.C. This is one of the most famous feats in ancient history.

In 490 B.C., Darius I, king of the Persian Empire (522-486 B.C.), wished to extend his hegemony to the Aegean Sea and mainland Greece. To do this, his army first occupied Thrace and Macedonia, then headed towards the city of Athens. The Persian king was indeed driven by his desire to punish the Greek cities, which were guilty of having supported the Ionians, who revolted against Persia in 499 B.C. After having conquered and looted several islands in the Aegean Sea, Datis, commander of the Persian fleet, landed his troops in the plains of Marathon (on the east coast of Attica, about 40 kilometers from Athens). After five days of facing one another, the Persian army was defeated and had to return to Minor Asia.

From then on, the Athenian propaganda appropriated the battle and turned this victory into a mythical event, by extolling the courage of the hoplites (foot soldiers of Ancient Greece), who fought, risking their lives to defend their land and maintain their independence.

GOOD TO KNOW

There are very few ancient sources on this period. As the Persians did not leave any written testimony of their history, the main sources are Greek: therefore, we are dependent on *The Histories* by Herodotus (Greek historian, 484-420 B.C.) and *Bibliotheca historica* by Diodorus Siculus (Greek historian, 90-30 B.C.). The story of the Greco-Persian Wars told by Herodotus, dating from 445 B.C., constitutes the most contemporary source to the facts. To write this book, the historian used several Attic, Spartan and Ionian oral sources that he collected during his travels. Despite some approximations and the liberties taken with regards to reality, *The Histories* remains a valuable book, which attempts to clarify the events in the light of the Greek and Persian perspectives.

POLITICAL AND SOCIAL CONTEXT

The Battle of Marathon took place during the Greco-Persian Wars (490-479 B.C.). It was the culmination of a conflict between some Greek cities and the Persian Empire.

The conflict can be broken down into three parts:

- The expansion of the Persian Empire (6th century B.C.);
- The revolt of Ionia and its repression (499-497 B.C.);
- The Aegean strategy of Darius I (491-490 B.C.).

EXPANSION OF THE PERSIAN EMPIRE

In the early 5th century B.C., the Persian Empire extended from modern day Pakistan to the Mediterranean coast and Egypt. Eager to expand his possessions, Cyrus II the Great (Persian king, c. 556-530 B.C.) defeated the Greek colonies in Minor Asia, called the Ionian cities, around 550 B.C.

Around 513 B.C., his successor Darius I reorganized his vast empire by creating provinces (called satrapies) and building two administrative cities: Susa and Persepolis. Keen to make further conquests, he gained new territories by invading the Indus Valley (Northern India).

Once his eastern base was consolidated, Darius I turned to the Black Sea, where he wanted to extend his influence to control the trade of precious metals, wheat and wood. He then began a series of conquests by taking the cities of Thrace and defeating the kingdom of Macedonia. Thrace gave him considerable benefits, as the area was rich in forests and silver mines. The Persians also gained control of two strategic straits:

- The Hellespont (Dardanelles) and the islands that controlled its entry (Imbros and Lemnos);
- The Bosphorus and the ports of Byzantium and Chalcedon (city of Minor Asia).

From then on, the empire controlled maritime traffic between the Aegean and the Black Sea. The Athenians, eager to dominate the lucrative market of the Black Sea, also established colonies at the Hellespont. Therefore, the progress of the Persians towards the west jeopardized their desires, soon causing a rivalry to rise between them.

To perfect his economic domination, the Persian king attacked the Scythians (settled north of the Black Sea, in South Russia) who were constantly earning wealth thanks to the trade relations they had with the Greek cities. However, he failed in his defeat and was forced to retreat. He then turned to the conquest of Greece.

THE IONIAN REVOLT

Darius I sailed to mainland Greece with the intention of defeating Athens and Eretria, as well as dominating the periphery of the Aegean Sea. In addition, he wanted to avenge the cities that had come to the aid of the Ionians during their revolt against the Persians.

Ionia (the western coast of modern day Turkey) was composed of a dozen autonomous cities, all subject to

Persian power from 540 B.C. They were able to retain their language, religion and customs, but were governed by the tyrant nominated by the Persian king. One of the cities, however, had a special status that gave it some independence: Miletus. Nonetheless, despite its relative autonomy, it also suffered from the Persian commercial dominance in the Aegean. Thus, as royal taxes increased, the Ionian cities grew indignant and expressed their desire for emancipation. They were also weakened economically by the limited trade in the Aegean, especially since the capture of Byzantium.

Therefore, Aristagoras, the tyrant of Miletus (late 6th century B.C.), proposed to the Persian satrap of Lydia that he conquer the Cyclades (Greek archipelago of the Aegean Sea) in the name of the empire; however, he did not honor his commitment. Driven by the fear of being assassinated or deposed, Aristagoras encouraged the people of Miletus to revolt. He proclaimed equal citizenship (called Isonomia) for Miletus and for all of the Ionian cities, which, therefore, chased away their tyrants. Aristagoras found military aid in Athens and Eretria – which was limited, but official – to face the Persian army.

GOOD TO KNOW

Isonomia (from the Greek *isos*, meaning "equal" and *nomos*, meaning "law") refers to the equality of citizens before the law. This notion appeared with Cleisthenes (Athenian statesman, second half of the 6th century B.C.) in the reforms introduced in 508-507 B.C. This political upheaval established the foundations of Athenian democracy, namely by strengthening the power of the ecclesia, a sovereign assembly that exercised legislative power and in which any citizen could participate. When revolts began against Darius I, Miletus therefore followed in the footsteps of Athens. This did not please the Persians at all, who had become accustomed to installing tyrants at the head of the Greek cities and were fundamentally opposed to the democratic conception of politics.

For six years, fighting raged. The Ionians won the first battles, and in 497 B.C., other cities began to revolt, such as Cyprus and Thrace. However, these cities definitively lay down their arms in 494 B.C. Miletus, lacking resources to power its fleets and mercenaries, found itself alone in facing the enemy. That same year, the city was attacked and a year later, the last islands were once again defeated by the Persian army.

The victory of his army awakened the expansionist desires of Darius I, or at least his willingness to establish regimes that would be in his favor in Greece. The role played by Athens and Eretria during this revolt ended up convincing him to impose his authority on both shores of the Aegean Sea.

THE AEGEAN STRATEGY OF DARIUS I

The failed campaign of 492 B.C.

Darius I organized a first expedition against Greece in 492 B.C. Herodotus reports that in the spring, the Persian king sent his son-in-law, Mardonius (died in 479 B.C.) to Minor Asia in order to gather their troops and lead them to Thrace to restore the authority lost in the Ionian revolt. The land army crossed the Hellespont and defeated the Macedonian, Thracian and Phrygian people, but the fleet, which was heading towards Acanthus, suffered heavy losses during a storm near Mount Athos. Mardonius then ordered a withdrawal of troops, which led to him being temporarily relieved of his role as commander.

The expedition of 491 B.C.

The following year, Darius I prepared a new campaign. He sent royal heralds (also called ambassadors) to many Greek cities to ask for "earth and water" (Herodotus The Histories, Book V: 17) as a sign of submission. Athens and Sparta refused and killed the Persian ambassadors, which was equivalent to a declaration of war.

In response, Darius I mobilized his land and naval forces and placed them under the command of Admiral Datis and General Artaphernes, who received, according to Herodotus, the "mission to enslave them and bring their people into his presence" (Herodotus, Book VI: 94).

He then set up an Aegean strategy to defeat the Greek islands before reaching Athens and Eretria: this was a success.

The two largest islands, Delos and Naxos, were seized without violence. From there, the conquest of the remaining islands was simple and the Persian army managed to easily defeat the Cyclades. The goal of Darius I was achieved. He eliminated any competition at sea before approaching the coast.

Landing on the island of Evia, the battle for the seizing of Eretria by the Persian fleet marked a bloody and murderous episode of the expedition. Facing the enemy alone, the city was besieged for six days, after which the city was looted and burned. Citizens were then deported to Susa, the capital of the Persian king.

Advised by Hippias, the deposed Athenian tyrant who found refuge with the Persians, Datis accosted his troops in the plains of Marathon on 13 September 490 B.C. After the announcement of this intrusion, the Athenians were joined by the Plataeans and set off to rescue them. The Spartans were also called upon, but the celebration of a religious festival required them to wait ten days before setting off on the road and when they reached the battlefield, the battle was already over. The Athenians therefore found themselves almost alone against the Persians when the battle broke out. However, Datis chose not to deploy all of his troops in the plains and sent a part of the cavalry to Phalerum, one of the three ports of Athens, in order to quickly capture the city.

The dating of the Battle of Marathon is still approximate today. Two dates are usually stated: 12 and 13 September 490 B.C., the latter being the most commonly accepted by historians. This date is the day of the landing of the Persian troops in the plains of Marathon.

COMMANDERS AND LEADERS

MILTIADES, ATHENIAN GENERAL

The son of Cimon Coalemos (Athenian Olympic champion, died in 524 B.C.), Miltiades belonged to a long line of Athenian aristocrats: the Philaids.

He became archon in 524 B.C., and from 518 B.C. he was responsible for the administration of the Thracian Chersonese (Thracian region governed by Athens) and was directly subjected to the Persian tutelage over the region. During the expedition led by Darius I against the Scythians, Miltiades was forced to campaign by his side, leading a contingent of the fleet. This experience taught him many things about the Persian military operations which would be of great help to him in the Battle of Marathon.

GOOD TO KNOW

The Philaids were a family closely related to the exercise of tyranny. Miltiades led the Chersonese of Thrace in a very authoritarian manner. His ancestor Cypselus (657-627 B.C.) was also the first tyrant of Corinth. Therefore, Athenian propaganda somewhat diluted the truth: Miltiades certainly saved democracy in Marathon, but he did not fight to defend this idea.

In 499 B.C., Miltiades was not involved in the Ionian revolt, but took the opportunity to reconquer the islands of Lemnos and Imbros that were previously under Persian rule. Fearing the vengeance of Darius I, he fled to Athens in 492 B.C., where he became leader of the oligarchic party (a form of government in which authority is in the hands of a few individuals) and was elected general two years later.

When the Persians invaded Marathon, he decided not to wait for the enemy behind the walls of Athens and set out with the Athenian hoplites towards the city. Moreover, he held important information as he knew about the Persian weaponry and therefore knew that the Athenians were better equipped for a hand-to-hand fight. After five days of facing one another, he decided to launch an attack, despite his lack of Spartan reinforcements. By doing this, he tried to gain time to join Athens, which was also threatened. The victory at Marathon earned him success, but his fame did not last long: he was wounded during the expedition he launched on his own against Paros (wealthy Cycladic island) and ended up being defeated. The consequences of this were serious: the Athenian Democratic Party accused him of treason for having led a personal expedition with the army of the city. Miltiades was then sent to prison. Unable to pay the fine, he died in prison in 489 B.C.

CALLIMACHUS OF APHIDNA, ATHENIAN POLEMARCH

There are very few sources that discuss Callimachus of Aphidna. This Athenian polemarch (army chief who also had religious functions) was born in the 6th century B.C. and died in 489 B.C., thus leaving very few traces.

However, it appears that he played an important role in the Battle of Marathon. Indeed, Herodotus states "Miltiades thus addressed him. 'Callimachus, he said, the fate of Athens in now in your hands; it is depending on you to enslave it, or set it free by acquiring immortal glory [...]'. The polemarch, encouraged by this speech, joined the position of Miltiades and his vote was decisive: it was resolved to launch the attack" (Herodotus, Book VI: 109-110).

During the battle, Callimachus of Aphidna became head of the right wing, as stated by Athenian law. While the center of the Greek military presence was defeated, the wings emerged victorious. His leadership was therefore of paramount importance for the victory. However, he died in battle after a valiant fight, according to the testimony of Herodotus.

DATIS THE MEDE, PERSIAN ADMIRAL

Datis the Mede, born in the late 6th century and died in the early 5th century B.C., also left very little trace of his life before 491 B.C.

That year, he was appointed head of the Persian fleet by Darius I and led the conquest of the Cyclades successfully. He also participated in the taking of Eretria alongside Artaphernes.

Herodotus states that he then attended the landing of Persian troops in the plains of Marathon. However, confronted with the defeat, he decided to take to the sea again with his trireme (Greek warrior ship with three rows of bunk rowers and rams) and head back to sea to bring his troops to the port of Phalerum (Athens port).

ARTAPHERNES, PERSIAN GENERAL

A Persian nobleman born in the late 6th century B.C., Artaphernes was the nephew of Darius I. His father was the satrap of Lydia, a region affected by the Ionian revolt.

In 491 B.C., Darius I ordered him and Datis to lead the Persian troops to conquer Greece.

A year later, Artaphernes participated in the capture of Eretria, which he looted and burned and he submitted the population to slavery. Herodotus makes no reports about his behavior at the Battle of Marathon. The only thing that is certain is that he was defeated by Miltiades and was thus forced to retreat.

In 480 B.C., he participated in the second Greco-Persian War organized by the successor of Darius I, Xerxes I (Persian king,

486-465 B.C.), but he occupied a subordinate position. He died in the early 5th century B.C.

ANALYSIS OF THE BATTLE

CHOOSING MARATHON

The Persians intended to defeat the city of Athens after their success in Eretria. However, instead of attacking the city directly, they chose to land their troops in Marathon, located 40 kilometers from the Greek capital. Thus, attracting the Athenian army near the city, Datis left the way open for the rest of his fleet, which was able to land safely in Phalerum. In this regard, it should be noted that the Greek coast was renowned for its mountains and valleys, which provided real protection and thus made the landings complex.

Herodotus reported that it was Hippias who advised Datis to land in the plains of Marathon. He added that the former tyrant also participated in the military campaign alongside the Persians. Therefore, the choice of location can be clearly explained: the plains of Marathon were part of the possessions of the Pisistratides, the family from which Hippias originated. He therefore wanted to seize it before leaving to conquer the throne of Athens, which he had been wanting to recover since his exile in 510 B.C.

The plains of Marathon.

ATHENS: A MILITARY DEMOCRACY

In Athens, military training was compulsory for all male citizens of 18-20 years. Once this was completed, any soldier aged between 21 and 59 could be called upon to fight.

After the land reform of Solon (Athenian statesman, 640-558 B.C.) in the 6th century, there were four classes of citizens divided according to their agrarian income. It was this social organization into census classes that prevailed in the allocation of different weapons:

- The Pentacosiomedimni, the wealthier citizens, served in the cavalry;
- The Hippeis and the Zeugitai formed the hoplites (heavy infantry), but some Hippeis who were rich enough could possess a horse and thus be part of the cavalry;
- The Thetes, who were landless laborers, were deployed

in the light infantry and the navy (which was underdeveloped in 490 B.C.).

The army was not permanent. It was called upon as required after the vote of the ten generals. In the case of Marathon, Herodotus states that they were not all in agreement: five were of the opinion that they should not fight, while the remaining five supported the conflict. The 11th vote, that of the polemarch, was decisive. It was Miltiades who convinced Callimachus to vote for the mobilization of the troops. In Athens, war was decided by a vote, not by the will of one man as in the case of Persia.

GOOD TO KNOW

The military hierarchy was closely linked to the life of the city and the officers, who were often elected for political rather than strategic reasons, were liable to a death sentence, exile or a fine in the case of defeat. Originally, the commander in chief of the army (the polemarch) was selected from the nine archons. Subsequently, this role was given to the generals, who divided the commands of the hoplite regiments between themselves. Their role changed, until they were allocated the supreme command of the army and the navy.

THE FORCES PRESENT

The Greek army

The exact figures are not known, but it is generally accepted that the Greek army raised 11 000 hoplites for the Battle of Marathon, of whom 1 000 were Plataeans. A third of Athenians of the age to be mobilized were called upon – the remaining two thirds were probably too poor to serve in the phalanx. Some historians argue that the army was mobilized hastily for fear of the return of the tyrant to the city. For fear of being too few, slaves were enrolled in the army for the first time.

The Athenian troops were led by ten generals (one for each tribe) and the polemarch, who all dealt with the command of the army in turn. According to Herodotus, some generals left to join Miltiades, who knew the Persian army well after having fought at its side against the Scythians.

The Persian army

It is also difficult to estimate the exact number of men who participated in the Battle of Marathon on the Persian side. Several authors reporting after the events mention a force of about 100 000-600 000 men. Added to this number are the triremes (warships), estimated at approximately 600 by Herodotus. These figures should be analyzed carefully and one should consider that they have been exaggerated for various reasons. Contemporary historians meanwhile argue the figure to be closer to 25 000 men and 1 000 horsemen. One should remember that the Persian army landed only a part of its troops in Marathon, leaving the others to head towards the port of Phalerum. However, it is still reasonable to assume that the forces of Datis and Artaphernes were double in size to the Greek army.

The army being composed of men from all corners of the empire, the soldiers did not all speak the same language and yet had to fight together. This multilingualism could have disadvantaged the Persian army during their maneuvers, even if it was organized according to the origins of the combatants. From Herodotus, we know that the Persians and the Saces (Scythian people) fought at the center of the military structure.

THE GREEK ADVANTAGE IN WEAPONRY AND THE LACK OF PERSIAN HORSEMEN

The weaponry of the Athenian hoplites was an advantage for the Greek army. They made up what was known as a heavy infantry and were very well equipped. They possessed:

- bronze helmets, shields, armor, greaves and armbands for protection;
- swords, long spears and shields of skin and metal to fight.

Traditional weaponry of the Athenian hoplites.

However, the weaponry of the Persian infantry was much lighter and proved less effective in the face-to-face fighting. In fact, they only had wicker shields and short spears. The Persian army was more known for its formidable cavalry, but few riders took part in the Battle of Marathon. At first glance, the plains seemed favorable to the deployment of horses, but upon visiting the battlefield, historians have realized that this was absolutely not the case. The admiral Datis therefore must also have realized this.

THE STRATEGY

Once they discovered that the Persian army was approaching Marathon, the Athenians left their city to go and meet the enemy. While the Persian infantry and cavalry landed in the plains, the Greek hoplites encircled the enemy to contain them on the beach and prevent them from reaching the city. They then positioned themselves on the heights of the plains to await the Spartan reinforcements. Unfortunately, a religious holiday forced the Spartans to wait until the full moon (which was 15 September) before they could leave.

After five days of facing each other and not receiving the arrival of reinforcements, Miltiades decided to launch the attack. He knew that the Athenian infantry was better equipped and could win a face-to-face combat. Also, their fighting technique, called Phalanx, was daunting: the hoplites set out in tight rows and were equipped with large shields which together formed a wall.

GOOD TO KNOW

The Phalanx technique of the hoplites was both a strategic formation and the implementation of a political ideal in the military sphere. According to Herodotus, it consisted of only the citizens of the middle class, owners who were represented in the assembly of the people. They were therefore guarantors of the Athenian civil spirit and were uniquely able to defend the land of their ancestors. They symbolized the victory of the affluent man, reluctant to share civil rights with the popular class. By winning a victory against the Persians, they confirmed the continuity of the body of citizen soldiers.

THE DEVELOPMENT OF THE BATTLE

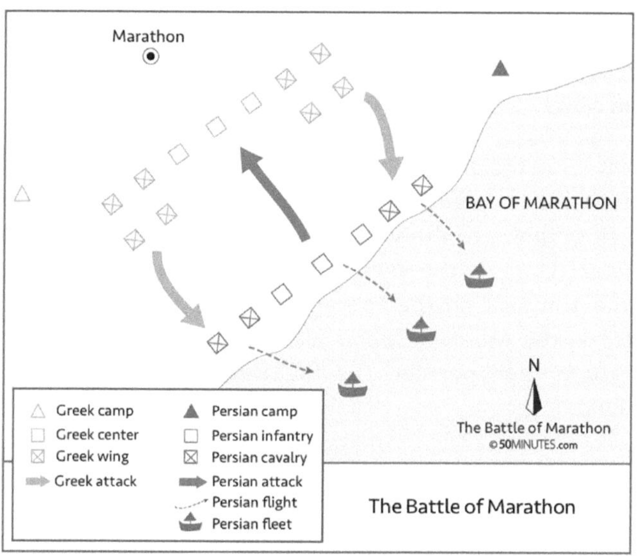

The Battle of Marathon

After five days of observation, it is unclear what prompted Miltiades to decide to launch the attack.

Several hypotheses exist:

- the departure of the Persian cavalry left a light infantry in place, which is likely to have pushed the Greeks to take action;
- Persians took an offensive stance, forcing the Greeks to lead the attack;
- the Greeks needed to end the Battle of Marathon as quickly as possible in order to rally the city that was vulnerable to Persian attack in the port of Phalerum.

Being outnumbered, the Greeks decided to strengthen their wings and reduce the forces in the center, while the Persian forces were evenly distributed in the center and on the wings.

Only 1 500 meters stood between the two armies when the Athenians stormed. The Greek hoplites first walked forward in close ranks, to the sound of flutes, and ran the last 100 meters towards the enemy to avoid arrows and cause a violent impact on the Persian line. Despite this powerful attack, the Athenian center was crushed and beaten. The Persians then pursued the fugitives who were heading inland.

A LEGENDARY RACE

Meanwhile, Callimachus and the Plataeans won a victory over the wings of the Persian army, forcing them to flee back to their ships. The Greek wings then turned against the Persian center and pursued those trying to join their vessels.

According to Herodotus, no less than 6 400 Persians were killed, while the Greeks only counted 192 dead, among which was the polemarch Callimachus. Moreover, the Greeks seized and burned seven Persian ships. Again, it is important to note that these figures should be considered with caution. Indeed, the number of Athenians killed seems very low considering the fact that their center was defeated. However, this gap between the two armies served to magnify the Greek victory even more.

Legend has it that when victory was announced, a messenger ran from the plains of Marathon to Athens to bring the news, travelling approximately forty kilometers. When he arrived at his destination, he died of exhaustion. According to Plutarch (Greek writer, 46-120 A.D.), the messenger would have been Eucles, but other sources speak of Pheidippides. Centuries later, an athletic event was created by Michel Bréal (French linguist, 1832-1915) to commemorate this feat: the marathon (42.195km run), which is the longest athletics event in the Olympic Games.

The Soldier of Marathon by Luc-Olivier Merson, 1869.

Once the battle was over, the Greek hoplites were to go without delay to Athens to counter the Persian attack at the port of Phalerum. Running, the troops arrived at the port after eight hours, just ahead of the Persian fleet. Seeing the path blocked, Datis decided not to land his troops and returned to Minor Asia.

This abandonment cast doubts on the importance of a conquest of Athens in the eyes of Darius I. The emperor perhaps wished only to lead a punitive expedition against a city that had rebelled against his authority.

REPERCUSSIONS OF THE BATTLE

THE VICTORY OF THE ATHENIAN DEMO-CRACY OVER TYRANNY

With the Persian defeat, the Battle of Marathon was also a sign of Hippias' failure. Athenian victory was celebrated as a liberation because it definitively eliminated the risk of tyranny returning to the city.

GOOD TO KNOW

After the departure of Hippias and the end of tyranny (510 B.C.), it was the aristocratic families of Athens who shared political power. Two years later, Clisthenes reformed the system and granted the people's participation in decision and policy functions. Citizenship was open to men over 20 years of age who were born to citizen parents and who had completed their two years of military service.

This victory quickly became symbolic and gave great prestige to Athens. Indeed, it convinced the Greek cities of their ability to triumph over the Persian enemy. Thus, during the second Persian invasion (480 B.C.), the Greeks felt able to fight the Persian army once again.

The victory was also a military one, as it highlighted the role of citizen-soldiers (hoplites) as defenders of the city and of democracy. The isonomic model was thus proved and was permanently registered in Athenian politics. Therefore, the rights of the affluent middle class were recognized. However, it was not until the second Greco-Persian war (480-479 B.C.) that the poorest citizens (Thetes) made their entrance onto the political and military scene thanks to the victory of Salamis (29 September 480 B.C.).

This success quickly became an ideological justification of the Athenian power and politicians used it to justify their hegemony over the Greek world.

The Persians lost the Battle of Marathon, but this defeat remained minor. Indeed, during the expedition of 490 B.C., Darius I managed to defeat the Cyclades and Eretria, which allowed him to dominate the Ionian cities, Thrace and the Hellespont. The Aegean Sea was under his control and consequently the main aim of the Persian Empire was achieved. Darius I wanted to quickly seek revenge, but a revolt broke out in Egypt (486 B.C.) which occupied him in the last months of his life.

THE FOUNDING OF THE DELIAN LEAGUE

As the Persians still posed a threat, the Delian League was founded in 478 B.C. This was a military alliance created by Athens to repel the Persians. Therefore, several Greek cities were grouped under Athenian authority:

- the islands of the Ionian Sea
- the Aegean islands
- the cities of Minor Asia.

The League gradually evolved into a state confederation, over which Athens imposed its supremacy. Athens received troops, ships, and also a tribute in silver from its allies, and in turn was committed to protecting the small cities with the help of Sparta.

THE SECOND GRECO-PERSIAN WAR

In 486 B.C., Xerxes I succeeded his father Darius I and, six years later, he led a punitive expedition to take revenge on Athens. He prepared his campaign for a long time and left nothing to chance. Xerxes planned to send two armies simultaneously to Athens:

- the first was to reach the city by land, crossing the Hellespont and Thrace;
- the second was to land from the sea.

Athens received support from many Greek cities and raised an army which remained largely inferior in number to that of the Persian king. However, the case of some cities such as Thebes should be mentioned, as they joined the Persian side for fear of reprisals.

When hostilities began, the Greek decided to occupy Thermopylae, a defensive position that provided access to the interior of their land. Unfortunately, they lost the battle and the Persians advanced on Athens, which was then abandoned by the majority of its inhabitants. The Acropolis was ransacked.

The famous Battle of Thermopylae took place in August 480 B.C. and the Persian troops opposed the Greeks. It took place in the Greek mountains, more precisely in the passage of Thermopylae, on the winding mountain road that connected the Thessaly to the plains of Attica.

The Greek coalition was led by Leonidas I (king of Sparta, died in 480 B.C.) who knew that the Persians had to take that route in order to stay in contact with their fleet. However, the king of Sparta was betrayed by one of his own who showed the Persians a path that would bypass the Thermopylae. When he discovered the betrayal, Leonidas I decided not to run away and to fight the enemy with part of his troops. He stood against the Persian army for three days, but was killed along with his army on the orders of Xerxes.

The Greek fleet decided to flee Attica and seek refuge in Salamis (small island south of Athens), but they were pursued by the Persians who followed them in the strait. Their large vessels impeded each other in the narrow passage and the Persians were dealt a bloody defeat. Faced with the loss of many ships, the few survivors retreated.

The naval battle of Salamis took place in September 480 B.C. near the small island of Salamis, located off Piraeus, an Athenian port. It was fought between the Greek and Persian fleets. The latter suffered a major defeat due to the strategy implemented by its opponent. Indeed, the 200 Greek triremes present encircled the Persian vessels in the strait and sank half of the enemy fleet. Xerxes I was forced to give up battle and save the rest of his fleet.

Xerxes I headed back to Persia but left his troops to spend the winter in mainland Greece. In the spring of 479, the general Mardonius launched the attack in Attica and occupied Athens. Soon, he was faced with a formidable Greek army in Boeotia. The Greek victory was completed at Plataea, and the Persian fleet was defeated.

The Battle of Plataea took place in 479 B.C. in Boeotia. It was fought between the Greek and Persian troops who had built a fortified camp at Plataea. The Greeks (Sparta, Athens, Corinth and Megara) raised a powerful army and marched on their camp. By choosing better positions, the Greeks gave the Persians the impression that they were retreating. Therefore, the Persians decided to pursue them, but were eventually defeated. The Persians who had remained in the camp were also killed. This battle ended the presence of Persian troops in Greece.

Other battles were fought by the Greeks in order to take over the Hellespont and the Aegean islands. In 499 B.C., the Peace of Callias was signed and ended the conflict: from then on, Athens dominated the Aegean world. The treaty also ended the Delian League, which no longer had a purpose. Athens, however, strengthened its domination:

- the treasure of Delos was transferred to Athens;
- Athenian colonies were founded in different cities;
- the use of its currency and its weight and measurement units was required;
- judicial authority was transferred to Athens.

THE ORIGINS OF DEMOCRATIC DISCOURSE

The day after the victory, Marathon was used by the Athenian Democratic Party, which made the fight against the Persians a symbol of the struggle for the freedom of the Greeks. From then on, Athenian literature and theater constantly exalted the courage of those who fought at Marathon. *The Persians* (472 B.C.), a famous tragedy by Aeschylus (Greek tragic poet, 525-456 B.C.), portrays Darius I and his relatives, collapsing as they hear the news of the defeat and the new Athenian hegemony: the author greatly exaggerated the importance of the battle in order to announce the coming omnipotence of Athens.

Gradually, Marathon became the rallying cry of the Greeks,

the defenders of civilization and equality against the "barbarism" of the Persians. In the 4th century, when the king of Macedonia, Philip II (382-336 B.C.) and his son, Alexander the Great (356-323 av. J.C.) were preparing the expedition in Asia (340 B.C.), thinkers such as Isocrates (Greek orator, 436-338 B.C.) and Demosthenes (Athenian statesman, 384-322 B.C.) recalled the memory of the Battle of Marathon to motivate the Greek cities to resume the ancestral struggle with the common enemy. This conflict meant, in the minds of the ancients, the victory of the Europeans over the Asians.

Finally, the European Renaissance and the rediscovery of Greek texts nourished humanist philosophy and, later, that of the Enlightenment. Part of the criticism of absolutism (a political regime in which a person has all the power) and the call for democratic revolutions draws its material from the stories of the Athenian feats accomplished in the name of Isonomia. Certainly Marathon, and more generally, the Greco-Persian wars, were the basis for egalitarian philosophy, which led the American Revolutionary War (1763-1783) and the French Revolution (1789) in the West.

SUMMARY

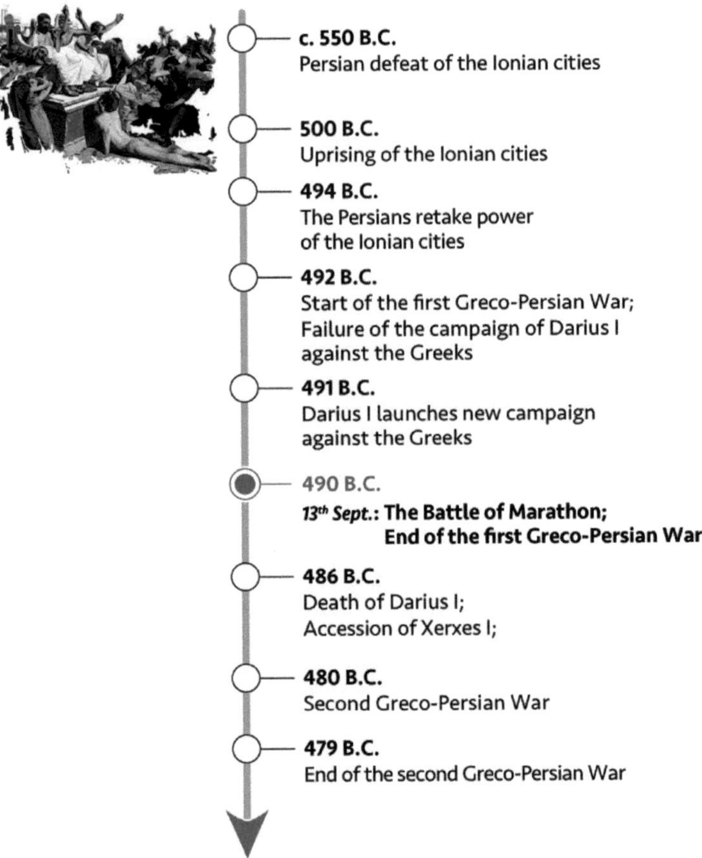

- In 500 B.C., a revolt broke out in Ionia in the Greek cities of Minor Asia that were dominated by the Persian

Empire. The movement was followed by others located in the Aegean Sea, but it was ultimately repressed by the Persians who recovered their domination in 494 B.C.

- Wishing to dominate Greece and extend his empire, Darius I noticed the economic interest that the domination of trade in the Aegean represented. Therefore, he launched a first campaign in 492 B.C., but this failed.
- One year later, he rethought his strategy and decided to conquer the Greek islands in the Aegean Sea to weaken the Greek trade.
- The Persian emperor was victorious over the Cyclades and tried to get into Attica by landing his troops in the plains of Marathon. Despite their numerical superiority, the Persian troops were defeated. It paid the price of less efficient equipment, compared to that of the Greek hoplites, and of the Greek strategy that forced them to bend. The Persians therefore had to retreat.
- For Athens, this was an important military victory that supported the democratic political model introduced recently (late 6th century B.C.). It announced the legitimacy of Athens to all the Greek cities that gathered around it with the Delian League in 478 B.C.
- For the Persian Empire, the defeat was minor as it already dominated a vast territory (from Egypt to the Ganges). However, Darius I died in 486 B.C and could not take his revenge. It was his son, Xerxes I, who took over the fight and attempted to invade Attica in 480 B.C. The conflict ended in 479 B.C. at Plataea (in Boeotia) with yet another Greek victory.

FIND OUT MORE

BIBLIOGRAPHY

- Aristophanes (1988) *Wasps*. Edited with introduction and commentary by MacDowell, D.M. Oxford: Clarendon Press.
- Billows, R.A. (2010) *Marathon: How One Battle Changed Western Civilization*. London: Gerald Duckworth.
- Briant, P. (2001) *Darius, les Perses et l'empire*. Paris: Gallimard.
- Briant, P. (2003) *From Cyrus to Alexander: A History of the Persian Empire*. Indiana: Eisenbrauns.
- Brun, P. (2009) *La Bataille de Marathon*. Paris: Larousse.
- Herodotus (2003) *The Histories*. Trans. De Sélincourt, A. London: Penguin.
- Laurén, G. (2014) *The Historical Library of Diodorus the Sicilian in Forty Books*. Sophron.
- Pausanius (1979) *Guide to Greece: Central Greece*. Trans. Levi, P. London: Penguin.
- Picard, O. (1995) *Les Grecs devant la menace perse*. Paris: Sedes.
- Will, E. (1989) *Le Monde grec et l'Orient, tome I : le Ve siècle*. Paris: Presses Universitaires de France.

ADDITIONAL SOURCES

- Green, P. (1998) *The Greco-Persian Wars*. Berkeley and Los Angeles: University of California Press.
- Krentz, P. (2010) *The Battle of Marathon*. New Haven: Yale University Press.

- Llewellyn-Jones, L. (2012) *Ctesias' History of Persia: Tales of the Orient*. Abingdon: Routledge.
- Lloyd, A. (2004) *Marathon: The Crucial Battle that Created Western Democracy*. London: Souvenir Press.
- Sekunda, N. (2005) *Marathon, 490 B.C.: The First Persian Invasion of Greece*. Westport: Praeger.

ICONOGRAPHIC SOURCES

- The plains of Marathon. Royalty-free reproduction picture.
- Tranditional weaponery of the Athenian hoplites. Royalty-free reproduction picture.
- *The Soldier of Marathon* by Luc-Olivier Merson, 1869. Royalty-free reproduction picture.

FILMS

- *The Giant of Marathon*. (1959) [Film]. Jacques Tourneur and Maria Bava. Dir. Italy/France: Titanus, Galatea Film, Lux Compagnie Cinématographique de France, Société Cinématographique Lyre.

IMPROVE YOUR GENERAL KNOWLEDGE

IN A BLINK OF AN EYE !

www.50minutes.com